MASTER YOUR message

Praises for *Master Your Message*

Do you have fears about letting your true personality shine through in your communication?

Do you find yourself defaulting to what you *think* you should say versus relying on your own voice?

Honestly, I still struggle with those things in my writing, podcasting, and speaking. Vernon's message is one that I personally needed to read and I'm glad he's written this book.

One of my favorite reminders in the book: it's *my responsibility* to ensure people understand me and my message. If I truly believe in my values, what I stand for, and what I want in life for myself and others, then I need to do my absolute best to ensure I can be understood.

I don't know about you, but I've got an important message I'm trying to deliver. I want people to experience freedom through improving their financial lives like I've been able to do and like so many people in my online community have done.

If more people heard that message, I'm convinced the world would be a better place.

What about you? What's your message? Do you know it well? If not, Vernon has you covered. He'll help you uncover that message.

Maybe you're like me and you know your message, but you're just not sure you're clearly communicating it and speaking from that authentic voice at the appropriate times.

I hope you'll use this book like I will: to sharpen your understanding of your own message and to have a better idea of when to deliver it with confidence.

Vernon's book is filled with revealing and captivating personal anecdotes that drive his message home. You'll enjoy learning from his life's lessons.

In all my dealings with Vernon Ross, he over-delivers when so many others use a "what's-in-it-for-me" first approach. If you're anything like me, I know you'll get extra value from his book.

> —**Philip Taylor**, AKA "PT Money," is the creator of FinCon, a community and annual event that brings together over 1,000 personal finance and investing influencers to help spread a positive money message.

You have a message that can inspire others if only you can discover it. I've known Vernon for a couple of years and he has a way of planting seeds in conversations that eventually can grow into new ventures or help you discover things about yourself and your business that were just out of view. In his book, *Master Your Message*, Vernon takes you through stories of others that have influenced him that will start you on the journey to finding your voice.

> —**Farnoosh Torabi**, *New York Times* Best Selling Author, Finance Expert and the creator of the So Money Podcast, Plutus Award winner of "Best Financial Podcast of 2016."

MASTER
YOUR
message

THE GUIDE
to Finding Your Voice
in Any Situation

VERNON ROSS

NEW YORK

NASHVILLE • MELBOURNE • VANCOUVER

MASTER YOUR message
THE GUIDE *to Finding Your Voice in Any Situation*

© 2017 **VERNON ROSS**

Published in New York, New York, by Morgan James Publishing. Morgan James and The Entrepreneurial Publisher are trademarks of Morgan James, LLC.
www.MorganJamesPublishing.com

The Morgan James Speakers Group can bring authors to your live event. For more information or to book an event visit The Morgan James Speakers Group at www.TheMorganJamesSpeakersGroup.com.

Shelfie

A **free** eBook edition is available
with the purchase of this print book.

CLEARLY PRINT YOUR NAME ABOVE IN UPPER CASE

Instructions to claim your free eBook edition:
1. Download the Shelfie app for Android or iOS
2. Write your name in **UPPER CASE** above
3. Use the Shelfie app to submit a photo
4. Download your eBook to any device

ISBN 978-1-68350-247-0 paperback
ISBN 978-1-68350-248-7 eBook
Library of Congress Control Number:
2016915446

Cover Design by:
Rachel Lopez
www.r2cdesign.com

Interior Design by:
Bonnie Bushman
The Whole Caboodle Graphic Design

Morgan James
The Entrepreneurial Publisher™

Builds

with...

Habitat
for Humanity®
Peninsula and
Greater Williamsburg

In an effort to support local communities, raise awareness and funds, Morgan James Publishing donates a percentage of all book sales for the life of each book to Habitat for Humanity Peninsula and Greater Williamsburg.

Get involved today! Visit
www.MorganJamesBuilds.com

A life story is written in chalk,
not ink, and it can be changed.
You're both the narrator and the
main character of your story.
—**Jonathan Adler**

DEDICATION

To my mother, Sallie—Without your constant showering of positive reinforcement, I would never have believed I could actually accomplish anything I set my mind to.

My sister, Renee—For being enthusiastic about everything I've ever wanted to do, no matter how crazy.

My wife, Jessica—For putting up with everything I am and taking this scary, crazy journey with me, and for loving me the way you do. I love you.

To my girls, Christina and Taylor—Books and your words are the things you leave behind. This work is for you and, as you grow older, your children and their children. I love you both more than anything in this world.

TABLE OF CONTENTS

FOREWORD

Have you ever corresponded frequently online with someone for years and never met them in person? I had tweeted back and forth with Vernon Ross for several years before I was blessed to finally meet him in real life at an event this year. It was like meeting an old friend. Like Vernon, I have a real passion and love for books. Growing up, I spent many hours immersed in the worlds created by other authors. There is nothing like holding a book in one's hands, flipping through and dog-earing pages and even sometimes highlighting insightful parts.

As I have grown through life experiences, my passion has grown into helping small business owners, entrepreneurs, and brands of all sizes harness the power of social media to build relationships and ultimately grow their businesses.

Like me, Vernon has this same passion for serving business owners. His passion is to help others find their voice—help others be who they authentically want to be. So, when Vernon asked me to write the foreword for *Master Your Message*, I was extremely honored.

Vernon has spent many years discovering and mastering his voice. He brings this knowledge and the evolutionary process to bear in his new book, *Master Your Message*. Vernon is an internationally known podcaster, author, social and digital strategist, and inspirational speaker who speaks from the heart and a place of real world experience. He speaks frequently on a variety of digital marketing topics at marketing conferences and workshops.

Have you ever thought that no one would want to hear what you have to say or that success is for other people and not you? Throughout the book, Vernon spends a lot of time helping his readers understand and accept their importance. Vernon draws upon personal experiences and stories to show his readers the importance of accepting and embracing their importance as a critical step in finding one's voice. His words, "You can't master anything until you get your thoughts under control," ring true, don't they? He stresses over and over again the importance of being who you want to be and not who people perceive you to be. Wow, that's a lesson we all need to learn!

Have you ever let fear hold you back from doing something you really wanted to do? Most people have a greater fear of speaking in public than they do of death! Have you ever been intimidated by the thought of speaking in public or in a social media live setting like Periscope, Facebook Live or even Podcasting? No need to worry. With chapters like *Fear, I Can't Stand How I Sound*, and *Intentional Conversations*, you will finish this book equipped with what you need to begin mastering that fear so that you can freely share your message with others.

If you are thinking, *"How am I going to overcome my fears and put myself out there on social media?"* you need to read this book. Understanding who you are and want to be and, more importantly, harnessing your fear, is imperative. You cannot have a successful social media voice and be effective without conquering and mastering your mindset.

This book goes into a lot of detail on how to overcome these fears, master your message, and find your voice in the sales process. You will learn the value of active self-expression and how to leverage digital platforms like podcasting and social media to build a responsive and profitable network.

Once you begin to understand how to find and master your voice, Vernon spends an entire chapter discussing how you master that voice on social media. Live stream marketing is a great tool, and I am a firm believer that this method of reaching customers is a match for any business. Not only does it increase engagement, but it dramatically increases your reach, especially in social media platforms like Facebook.

Take time to sit down and read this book cover to cover. Keep a highlighter or pen handy to highlight the nuggets you find within. The key to a finding your voice and mastering your message is in this book. Write down your thoughts and takeaways. It is through understanding who we are and who we want to be in life that we succeed at mastering our voice.

There is no reason you can't find your voice online, on stage, behind the mic, or in any situation and be the master of your voice and message. I know you will get a ton of value from this book!

—**Kim Garst**, CEO, Boom Social, International Best Selling Author of *Will the Real You Please Stand Up; Show Up, Be Authentic and Prosper in Social Media*, and *Success Secrets of the Online Marketing Superstars*.

THANK YOU

My very heartfelt thank you because, without your pushing, accountability phone calls, Skype messages, and introductions to all the right people over the past couple of years this book would have never happened. You've helped change my life and I'm forever grateful.

Jaree Freeman
Fabienne Raphael
Harry Duran
Chris Cerrone
Lacy Urcioli
Nick Pavlidis
Jared Easley
Dan Franks

PT and the Entire Fincon Family

Nina Babel

Brandy Butler

Karen Anderson

Morgan Gist McDonald

And every podcaster, guest, and friend I've met over the past three years.

INTRODUCTION

BOOKS MEAN SO MUCH TO ME

Books have always been the one thing I could go to for comfort and protection.

I grew up in one of the worst neighborhoods in St. Louis—the Northside. It wasn't uncommon to hear gunshots every night and to instinctively duck, or on New Year's Eve not to walk around when the clock struck midnight for the fear of being randomly shot, which almost happened one year. A bullet ripped through our front door, exploding into the steps leading upstairs just two steps below where my mother had just walked.

Adding to the situation, my college-educated mother would have no part of the public school system, so she sent both my sister and me to private school, despite having very little money and limited resources after my father, a Korean War veteran, passed away when I was just five years old.

Even though her decision to send us to private school was a great hardship, she enrolled me in a Catholic school called Our Lady of Perpetual Help, while my sister attended Cardinal Ritter College Prep. PH, as we called it, was just five blocks from our house, so I walked there most days.

Our Lady of Perpetual Help had been in the neighborhood for around a hundred years at the time and even had a full convent where the nuns lived. I loved my school but the walk there and back, morning and evening, wasn't always the best experience. When you're the only kid on your block going to a private school and everyone else is going to a public school life can be a little challenging.

Don't get me wrong, I had plenty of friends, but none of them walked in the same direction as I did, so if my sister wasn't walking with me to school it was almost a guarantee something silly would happen. Older kids mostly picked on me, but one time three other boys and I were held at gunpoint and told to give up our coats. Now, a good coat wasn't easy to come by, and honestly, in that moment I was more afraid of my mother than the guy standing in front of me. It turns out the gun wasn't real this time, and since he was just a teenager, my friends and I jumped him, took the BB gun, and gave him the business.

Like I said, life was challenging, and to escape that daily grind I would read, and read a lot!

I was blessed to be a gifted reader from an early age and loved to read everything, but I can't take credit for that love of reading alone. My mother read to me at an early age and there were always books in the house. If you ever wanted to know where I was hiding at school you could find me in the library. Bullies never hang out there, by the way, so it's always a good option if you're a book nerd.

The books took my mind off the sprinting I'd have to do between home and school in order to avoid the riffraff. My favorite book in those days was Rudyard Kipling's *The Jungle Book*. I so loved this book because I identified with Mowgli—an outsider to the animals he was raised around with no real desire to be with the humans he was "supposed" to embrace. Mowgli was more comfortable outside of where he discovered he belonged.

That was my daily struggle in my neighborhood and at school. I never felt I was truly a part of my neighborhood or my class. Every day when I read *The Jungle Book*, I would escape to the jungles of India to get away from the one I lived in. Books were truly my saving grace.

PODCASTING IS LIFE

Podcasting has really changed how I look at the world.

To truly understand what podcasting means to me and how it makes me feel, I need you to hold your breath. Really! Are you holding it?

If you are, are your lungs burning yet as your body fights your will to not breathe? Keep holding it and don't breathe until your body forces you to. Now breathe in deeply.

That's podcasting for me, and that's what speaking in front of people is to me. It's like breathing for the first time; or better, it's like coming up for air.

Having a great conversation with someone I'm connecting with on a podcast is a feeling like no other. I can only look at what I've discovered about myself this way.

When someone is called to serve Christ and is asked, "Why do you serve?" or, "How did you become a [priest, nun, reverend, etc.], they tend to answer the same way. "I had a calling, a yearning that was so strong I couldn't resist it. I knew in my heart it was the right thing to do so I had to answer the call."

That's how podcasting is for me. I come alive when I'm talking to a guest and get to learn who they are, what their unique stories are, and what things are important to them. I like to learn how they arrived at the point they're at in their lives.

When I connect with a guest it's like magic. I feel myself smiling from ear to ear, and though at times I'm emotionally exhausted when an interview is over, I love every minute of it. Is that mastering your message? In part, I think it's finding your calling and discovering your passion and finding your voice. Through podcasting and speaking and life experience, I've been able to find my voice.

WHY THIS BOOK? WHY NOW?

Let's start with the problem. I see people on a daily basis who don't know how to express themselves. Either they're afraid or just don't understand how to be themselves. I call it not *mastering your message*, which is how I came up with the title of this book.

What this means is when it's time for someone to speak up in a meeting or on their brand new podcast, or give an impromptu toast at a retirement party or wedding, they want to say the perfect thing but can't find the words, as much as they try. I think we've all had the fantasy when called upon to speak to deliver a speech that leaves the room erupting in cheers and standing ovations or moves them to tears as you walk proudly off the stage.

Don't get me wrong; I'm not going to give you a magical technique to help you nail every speech—I'm going deeper than that. I want to show you in this book how to develop the mindset and discover your voice so that even if you don't deliver a knock-them-dead speech or toast at the next event you attend, you'll be good with what you did deliver. I believe by the end of this book you will find true freedom and be on a path to discover your life's purpose.

I want you to see a world that helps you live the life you want by being true to who you are, understand what you stand for, and express it unapologetically.

Chapter 1

EMERGENCE

Our deepest fear is not that we are inadequate. Our deepest fear is that we are powerful beyond measure.
—Marianne Williams

WHO ARE YOU TO BE BRILLIANT?

Have you ever asked yourself that question? Haven't we all?

When stepping out of any darkness, our natural reaction is to shield ourselves from the light and to almost retreat back to where we came from. We've adjusted to it, just being able ɔ see and make our way around in it, but we know we have to eventually step into the light.

In *The War of Art*, Steven Pressfield calls it *going pro*. That's when you've gotten to the point of an activity in which you have to make a choice: continue to play a small game and keep the activity as a hobby or a side thing, or really jump in with both feet into the pool of whatever it is you've chosen.

Perhaps you think I'm going to talk about entrepreneurship, and that's partly true, but you can jump in with both feet into any number of things. Playing a bigger game could be as simple as going back to school to finish a degree, but you're fearful of becoming a student again because of your non-traditional status. Life isn't about business all the time, but life is about making choices that either move you forward or keep you right where you are.

So what's that got to do with asking yourself, "Who am I to be brilliant?" Who are you to want more, do more, or demand more? I think that's the real struggle we have to get past—the negative thoughts that keep us from stepping up to the idea of a unique message. As we move forward together, I'm going to talk more about how mastering your message will change your life.

Breaking the Mold

Often it's difficult to really express yourself outside of what's considered to be the conventional wisdom; the things you should or shouldn't do; the constructs of the expectations of the masses.

We tend to base what we do, who we are, and ultimately, what our message is, on the expectations around us.

Our deepest fear is not that we are inadequate. Our deepest fear is that we are powerful beyond measure. It is our light, not our darkness, that most frightens us.

—Marianne Williamson

Think about this fully. Are your feelings of inadequacy really keeping you from expressing who you are, or is it that you fear what you will become once you take a step toward your true self? I've experienced both. It's challenging to deal with and accept that fear can grip us, pulling us back into the darkness and telling us our refusal to conform is going to hurt our family or our career. These feelings can paralyze you and keep you stuck right where you are.

The other side I struggle with is when I absorb these words and envision how awesome life will be on the other side of this entire process. However, success often means realizing not everyone in your world is going to make the journey with you.

Understand those expectations actually serve as a way to protect you. I know it may seem counter to what everyone else may be saying about ignoring the haters and "*You-do-you" people,* but that's not really the space I'm writing about. You can and should fight convention, but that only gets you so far. Understanding what the motivation is might help you move past the judgmental behaviors and attitudes you're bound to run into as you embark on your mission to master your message.

It often starts with your friends and family telling you from a very early point what you can't do. Let's think tree climbing for a sec if, like me, you've ever tried to climb a tree just to have an adult tell you to get down because trees aren't made for climbing. Yes, I had someone tell me that, and I actually remember getting down and for a while I thought believed them. It wasn't because I was convinced they were right; it had more to do with this person being in a position of authority and I felt obligated to comply. It's a silly thought, really, that *trees aren't made for climbing.* I think that's why I ended up back in that same tree several times after that initial climb.

It's likely your first detractors will be family, then friends, and ultimately even people you don't know. Recently I had an interesting conversation with a friend about building her

LinkedIn profile to better align with her goals and her business. She was afraid to remove her current job from her profile, which is one of the tactics I recommend. She was afraid because she thought her connections would wonder why she removed her current job and proceed to ask too many questions about her business. She was afraid it would look unprofessional and it was possible her boss might see what she had done.

My response to her was this. It's not easy to break the mold and step outside of convention. You have to ask what your current job has to do with your business and whether having it on your profile aids in communicating your unique message to your audience. LinkedIn isn't a site for you to showcase things that aren't aligned with your values, goals, dreams, or your message. It's to showcase your professional experience to your peers and clients. Of course it's great for displaying your current experience and past employers to give others an idea of how you've gotten to where you are and where you want to go, but it's not for promoting content that doesn't serve you. So the conversation in my mind wasn't really about LinkedIn.

When it comes to mastering anything in life, it takes 10,000 hours to be good enough at anything to be considered an expert, as Malcolm Gladwell states in *Outliers, The Story of Success.*

I agree with that theory entirely. However, I think it may take that long or even longer to accept your own mastery and to start living it. For me it only took thirty years to accept my calling to help other people master their message. It's funny how things you think don't matter or didn't have an influence over you at one point in time turn out to have a profound influence when reflecting back over your life.

When reviewing material for this book I decided to include a letter a friend from my past sent after a youth retreat in the summer of 1986.

Hey there Vernon,

How's your fourth day? Is everything okay at school and home? You really freaked alot of us out Sunday night. You were pretty shy before then. But then you got up there and started talking. My jaw literally dropped. Then you pulled me up there totally unprepared. I had no idea what you wanted me to do. You are one really neat guy.

I'm sending you a map of our pictures. If for some silly reason you should forget a name or two, you can just look it up.

John wants everyone to bring softball equipment to the reunion. See you there.

2 Timothy 2: 6-13

Love in Christ,
Tony "Spaz" Haughey

Pretty interesting, right? What struck me while reading this letter was how he noticed how shy I was at first before I began speaking. This is one of the nicest letters I've ever received and one that I've often gone back to when I feel like I'm losing my way or not being true to myself.

> *They don't know you until they know you, so you may as well show them the person you want to be.*
> **—Vernon Ross**

So let's take a quick trip back to retreat weekend. My priest, Father Bob, invited me and one of the altar boys to a youth retreat. It was my first real time away from home, so I was a little afraid, especially when we arrived and I realized everyone there was white. I didn't (and still don't) have a problem being around white people, but that was the first time I would be spending the night with a group of total strangers.

I was already a pretty shy kid to begin with, so I didn't have much to say and only did what was required to not be a total hermit. The other kids were really great and did everything they could to make my friend Alex and me feel like part of the group. Alex took right to it and really participated. I, on the other hand, did a little so as not to be rude, but I didn't really get involved until the very last night.

We were split into groups to act out a play or scene of something that reflected on the Bible lessons we'd studied that weekend. I don't recall what the subject was, but I do recall that since I'd been so distant I felt once again that I was on the outside looking in at my life happening. Either way, I was chosen to be the host of a mock talk show concept we came up with. It was the first time I was ever in front of a group of people talking, other than reading something aloud at school.

Getting up off the floor in the huddle we were in, I was terrified, but that only lasted the first ten seconds or so as I walked to the front of the room, all eyes on me. As I walked up, all of a sudden it hit me and I thought of the movie *Risky Business*. Yes, the Tom Cruise flick that I watched on a bootleg recording at a friend's house a few weeks prior. We probably watched it three or four times that weekend.

I identified with Cruise's character, even though his life and world were pure fantasy to me. I was poor, living in the inner city, and attending a private school my priest was helping to pay for. I supplemented this charity, or grant, by working at the church every Saturday while my mother worked the rummage sales and food pantry. Nothing could have made me more different from Joel Goodsen, Cruise's character, but for some reason I connected with him.

I'm not sure what exactly hit me, but I remember thinking to myself, "What the Heck [F-Bomb]," just like in the movie. I decided to be who I wanted to be in that moment, and it wasn't a shy, black kid from the inner city who didn't belong with this group of white kids who had nothing in common with me, or so I thought. I wasn't going to be someone who was so afraid of being judged or laughed at by others that he wouldn't speak up. Instead, in that moment I was going to be an outrageous and over-the-top talk show host everyone would love.

I walked up, took a deep breath, turned around, and for the first time ever I was myself. I wasn't up on stage running around and riling everyone up for my sake; it was for them. My performance was funny and made everyone, including my group, laugh as I showcased everything we'd learned and experienced throughout that weekend. It was my montage moment—and I crushed it!

What I discovered from that experience is that at every turn in your life and every time you meet a new group of people, you have an opportunity to be exactly *who* you want to be and *how* you want to be.

If you want to be outgoing, then be outgoing. If you want to be confident, be confident. There's nothing to hold you back from being the person you want to be, even in the midst of strangers.

The incredible part is that as soon as you do this and have an experience in which you step into your greatness, it's really difficult to go back to being someone you really aren't. The people who have preconceived notions about you or have tucked you away into a neat little box will begin to notice the changes in you.

Mastering your message isn't about learning to deliver a talk or any other one-time experience; it's about mastering who you want to be in life and how amazing that experience is when you truly embrace it.

I learned so much that weekend about myself and what I was capable of by deciding to be the person I wanted to be and not just what people perceived me to be.

What People Think You Are, You're Not

Would you agree that most of us expect someone to sound a certain way based on how they look? I think it's safe to say we all make assumptions, right?

One of the first times I experienced an assumption of this kind, I directly influenced someone else's perception and expectations of me and my intent. It was fascinating to experience and to look back on that situation with the benefit of hindsight.

When I was young, I became an exercise enthusiast at an early age, thanks to my mom for buying a subscription to *Muscles and Fitness* magazine. Reading about working out lead to working out, which lead to hanging out in gyms. When I wasn't in the gym I would wander through the sporting goods stores, planning out my next purchase.

On this particular day, I decided to shop first for the motivation for what I wished I could buy. At seventeen, I was pretty light in the disposable income department, and my mother was using my social security benefit from losing my father when I was five to pay my thirty-five-dollar-a-month gym membership. She believed it was more important for me to be in an affluent area, working out and meeting new people, than to have that extra money each month. She knew my exposure to the world of affluence would shape how I looked at the real world based on the contrast between it and the world I lived in.

So, I was in the store looking at full leather workout belts and picturing Arnold (yes, *that* Arnold) advising me on which one to buy. I heard the heel on the door clang as a cop walked in. I glanced over at him then turned back around to continue my fantasy when I felt a hand on my shoulder. I looked up to see the cop standing over me. "Hey kid, what are you doing in here?" Before I could say a word, the store clerk called over to the officer, "Hey, Joe! He's okay!"

Officer Joe acknowledged her exclamation, but tightened his grip on his nightstick a little stronger and asked again, "I said, what are you doing here?"

I looked up smiled, "Hi, Officer. I'm on my way to Bodybuilder Inc. right up on Brentwood but wanted to stop here first to check out some gear." He looked surprised, so I continued. "Is everything ok, sir?" He removed his hand and asked, "So, where are you from?"

I must say I was a bit confused, and apparently my face showed it because the clerk interjected again. By now she was standing next to me. "Oh Joe, he's African!"

Now that was a shocker, because for a second I thought she couldn't have been talking about me.

"I'm sorry, but I'm not exactly African—as in, not from Africa—I'm from the north side."

"No way! You're so well spoken!" Officer Joe scoffed.

"Yeah, well, I go to Cardinal Ritter College Prep and some of the kids in my neighborhood do say I talk funny, or white."

Instantly, both the officer and the store clerk burst out laughing at what I'd said. You'd have thought I was Eddie Murphy the way they were roaring. When they finally finished laughing, the cop offered me a ride up the street to the gym. I accepted and we left together in his squad car. When we got to the gym, he decided to park the car and walked in with me. I suspect that although he was amused he still wanted to make sure I was actually a member there.

He was finally convinced when he saw the club manager and a couple of the gym rats greet me as I walked in. Officer Joe stopped to talk with the owner, whom he knew well, as I continued on to the locker room.

I don't recall that I ever shared the Officer Joe encounter with my mother, but as I've looked back on the situation I've realized the better you communicate and the more articulate you are, the more people are likely to respect you and be more willing to listen to what you have to say. I've continued to take that lesson forward in my adventures—and it's helped me greatly.

NOT AN AFTERTHOUGHT

As I write this book, the national news coverage is full of stories of black men being killed on the streets by police. When I look back my experience with Officer Joe, and every situation I've been in with the police, I've lost count actually. I've had the attitude and posture that I've done nothing wrong and have nothing to be fearful of. I haven't been negatively impacted, but that's not the case with everyone. I have three friends who have been impacted, and like me weren't doing anything but being black.

I wish it were the answer to this societal problem, but I fear it's not. I don't have the answers in this book to address this problem, but I think it would be irresponsible to not acknowledge that there is a problem and that as a country we need to find a solution.

Chapter 2

GET YOUR MIND RIGHT

We all have to start a little broken to build ourselves up.
—Vernon Ross

Developing a positive mindset is critical if you want to master your message. You can't master anything else until you get your thoughts under control. That last statement is powerful, but I can't think of anything that can be more difficult. In fact, while attempting to write this book over the past two years, I'll admit I've stopped more than I've started. That is actually possible. Here's how.

There were several times I wanted to crack open the laptop and start writing but I would talk myself out of it or come up with reasons to not start. The resistance was five to my one, which is the number of times outside of this writing when I've been serious about accomplishing this work. To fully understand the problem, I think you have to understand the root cause of the situation.

My first attempt at writing this book was in late 2014, but those two months of effort ended up with me in full mental breakdown mode, ugly cry and all. It was all about Brother John and what he'd said to my mother about me. Everything I had been holding down for years erupted. Until then I'd become pretty proud of the progress I'd made on the book up until that point; that is until I decided to actually read what I had written.

It was complete garbage. It's wasn't interesting and didn't capture one real idea in the entire thing. Eight thousand words of wasted space, time, and effort that I would never get back. To make things worse, I kept thinking Brother John was right; I'm nothing and I haven't amounted to anything. I'm a complete failure and fraud. A complete and total waste of space who's just wasting everyone's time with these silly dreams of becoming more. After all, I never even finished college.

Here's the context. In grade school, I was constantly bullied and ridiculed by a couple of behaviorally challenged young men. Unlike a lot of kids who were also bullied in school, I was willing to fight back and stick up for myself. I'm no victim and never have been, but if you were going to hit back you had to make sure that Sister Mary Katherine wasn't watching. Whenever she caught sight of us kids, I would be the one in trouble because I was the one hitting according to her perspective.

After about my fourth suspension from school, my mother was invited to go talk with Sister Adel, my teacher at the time, along with Brother John. After meeting with Sister Adel and Brother John, my mother discussed what happened from my perspective (I think she wanted to see if I would tell the same story) and what was expected of me.

I wish I could recount the entire conversation, but sadly I can't. What I do remember is my mother repeating to me what Brother John said to her. He'd said, "Ms. Ross, I'm just going to tell you that if Vernon continues to act the way he is now, he's not going to amount to anything."

"Ok," she answered in her in classic Sallie Ross way. Then she continued with me, "You know what Brother John told me? He told me, 'Your son ain't gonna amount to nothing, not the way he's acting. He's going to either end up dead or in jail.' Now the question I have for you is, are you going to prove him right, or are you going to grow up to be the man I know you can be?"

My mother always believed in me, no matter what. She encouraged me daily and reassured me that I was intelligent and could do anything, and I do mean anything, I put my mind to.

All of that still didn't seem to make a difference when I thought I had failed at writing. It wouldn't have been the first failure in my adult life, but for some reason it seemed to hurt more and cut more deeply than any time before. It took about an hour of non-stop sobbing before I could compose myself. I wasn't sure at the time what was going on or why this affected me so deeply, but what I did understand is that I needed to figure it out.

Then I was suspended again for fighting. Yes, suspended for fighting, but in reality, I was always the one getting beat up. It seemed I wasn't smart enough to know that if you're going to hit the person back, be sure to wait until the teacher isn't looking.

For years Brother John's words held me back—the underlying thought that maybe he was right, and for the longest time, I actually thought getting a great job and making a lot of money would prove he was wrong. I don't know why his opinion of me still mattered; I have no idea if the man is even still alive.

It's funny how the ghosts of the past remain in our lives and keep us from seeing what's right in front of us. Those hateful words of doubt from your childhood that bite you if you stare in the mirror too long or make you think you shouldn't when your gut tells you that you should catch that dream you've been chasing.

It came to me on a drive home just a few nights ago. I thought about Brother John and what my mother told me he'd said about me. I thought to myself and may have even said out loud, "You're right! I didn't amount to anything, I amounted to something! I'm a great father, a loving husband, and a good friend to many. I show kindness to people and I inspire them to do more and be who they are. Through podcasting and speaking, I've been able to help change or guide the direction of the people I touch. I'm something, Brother John, and I matter."

WELL, THAT SLOWED ME DOWN A LITTLE

It didn't stop me from writing, but I had so much growing to do over the next few months, and it ended up being an entire year plus some months before I got started again. What I think affected me so much about what was said is that I internalized the statement and measured everything in my life against proving to someone that honestly wasn't important. I didn't need to prove to Brother John or anyone else that I had amounted to something and that I mattered.

You never know what's going to change you and/or what's going to make a difference in your life and how you see yourself. For me, it's always been reading and even now it's listening to audio books along with writing in journals. It was Summer 2014 when I discovered a book called *The Four Agreements* by Don Miguel Ruiz. It's a book about the Toltec belief system. There's a section in the book that talks about how you shouldn't take anything personally, not even the things you think about yourself. That's when it happened—an actual lightbulb moment came to me while I was doing yard work.

I had already achieved everything I would ever need and none of it had to do with money or traditional success. I have two wonderful children who are both healthy and doing well in school and mostly well-adjusted to life. My wife Jessica is an amazing mother and great wife and our marriage is solid and stronger than ever. Once I understood and looked at what I really had achieved it was easier to actually sit down and start writing.

It was also a lot easier to start applying all the mindset coaching I've learned over the years to my own life and following the advice I had been giving to clients. Nothing feels worse as a coach than to know you're not fully embracing everything you're teaching, and what's worse is to not even realize that you weren't embracing it.

It's not that I wasn't aware my mindset wasn't right, but once I understood I was actually winning was when the breakthrough came, the process of getting my mind right to deal with whatever issues I would encounter when writing.

Often we aren't aware of the mindset issues that hold us back and I've found that we tend to put other things in the way of things we would have to face that move us forward.

A Practice I Started

I started this two-minute exercise whenever I notice my mindset is drifting to being overly critical or negative about life in general.

Grab a piece of paper and think about the mindset challenges you have right now. What makes you doubt yourself? Now write everything down that comes to mind. Is it real or self-imposed? Label each one accordingly.

Now review the list and ask this question. Are you allowing others to affect how you see yourself? Write down and take a close inventory of everything good in your life and focus on those things.

How You View Success Affects Your Mindset

When you think of success who do you picture? Maybe it's Jay-Z for what he's been able to do in business or Mark Zuckerberg for building the largest social network in history. We tend to picture the "greats" as to what success looks like. Followed by the thought, *I could never do something that great.*

How do you picture yourself? When I mentioned Jay-Z did you think, *I could never be better than Jay-Z or as wealthy as Elon*

Musk? What about someone you work with on a daily basis. Have you looked at one of your more successful co-workers and thought, *I could never sell as much or be that smart.* Do you feel dejected, as if success isn't something for you? Have you ever had that feeling?

You're not alone. Much of my life I never really believed I was successful. Although I was making ten times the income my mother ever made and could pretty much afford anything I wanted or go anywhere I wanted, I still wasn't. I always felt like I hadn't succeeded.

My problem was I never really defined what success actually meant to me, nor did I have a plan to achieve it. What I did have was a desire to not be the failure that one of my grade school teachers told my mother I would be on one of her countless visits to school to get me out of trouble.

I knew I wanted to provide for my family and work in the technology field. Honestly, that was enough to get me to where I was, but it wasn't fulfilling.

It wasn't until I found my voice through podcasting that I found that total fulfillment I never really had from my technology career. I've come to understood those past hurts were affecting how I was seeing myself. I had all the trappings of success but inside I still wasn't good enough.

Even though I had outward success, my internal conversations were coming from a place of doubt and not believing in myself. It would be easy to blame Brother John for how I was thinking but I'm the only person responsible for my thoughts and how I view myself, and you're the only one who can control how you think about yourself.

Some food for thought: People usually get what they think is possible. If you don't believe something is possible it's not very likely you'll achieve it.

Chapter 3

FEAR

WRITING THIS WAS SCARY

Actually writing this book was one of the scariest things I've had to do in my life. It wasn't as if I sat down thinking I was going to do more than self-publish and hopefully sell a few copies. Yes, the negative self-talk was in full-on, set-those-low-expectations mode. I think you know what I'm talking about. We've all been there.

When that thing happens—you know, the one you could only dream of happening—you want to run away and hide until it's all over, then go back and watch some Netflix. Can't have success before you're ready. Of course I'm poking fun at myself and illustrating how silly we can be even when good things happen in our lives.

Music can Reveal so Much

A few years ago I discovered a UK artist named Ben Howard while watching a YouTube video. I can't recall the video, but the song was amazing so I looked up the artist. After following him for about a year he came out with a song called *The Fear*. He laments through his singing about how he's been worrying he'll lose the ones he holds dear. The apathy will make a fool of us all. These were powerful words that spoke deeply to me at a time I need to push past fear and really start to go after what I wanted.

Let's explore how fear may be holding you back and preventing you from mastering your message and doing the things you've been dreaming about. Let's break through the confines of fear.

I've heard and actually researched that fear is designed to keep us safe because "the night is dark and full of terrors," as is said in *Game of Thrones*. When you're afraid you have a heightened awareness. Everything is hyper focused and even time seems to slow down.

We're going to use the feelings you get as a good indicator that you're on the right path and that what you're attempting to do and, of course, talk about is worthwhile, or else you wouldn't be afraid.

It's hard to start a business, and to even think about quitting your job to go do your own thing is absolutely terrifying. It's a real challenge, and along with that challenge often creeps in fear to let you know this isn't going to be a walk in the park. Fear grabs you like a hand on your chest pushing you so hard you can't breathe.

Everything you are tells you this is what you want, but fear tells you it's something you can't have. It makes it hard to think and paralyzes you. It can be so hard to pick up the phone and call that lead or talk to that event organizer you emailed and told you would call in the next week but it's now three weeks later and you haven't called yet. Deep breath.

Often it's so difficult to just take that first step because you don't know if it leads to the light. Speaking from experience, I know it's hard to get up on stage and talk to an audience. In fact, maybe you've heard the fear of public speaking is worse than the fear of death. Fear is a master at holding us back. But it's a natural thing and a very human behavior.

So How do You Push Past Fear?

You don't!

Fear isn't something you can ever get past, but like your message, you can master it and control your behavior around it. You can use it to control your emotions and get a grip.

I've learned to embrace fear because it's that sinking and excited feeling you get when everything around you is buzzing because you're about to do something that's unnatural and uncomfortable for you.

Embrace it and understand what your mind and body are telling you. It's saying take action despite that feeling because when you take action enough you get comfortable with taking action and understanding your feelings about this new and very scary thing you're doing.

It gets easier over time, but the feeling never really goes away. There are actually times when I search for that feeling to tell me I'm ready to go and do this thing, to get on stage and talk to a few hundred or even thousand people; it tells me everything is going to be awesome even though I'm afraid. I'm not going to mess up! I'm going to make sure I deliver! I'm prepared and I've done everything possible to make sure I rock the stage, deliver my message, and communicate greatness. That's what fear is telling me and that's what I'm telling you.

Here's an analogy. It's a little bit of Neural Linguistic Programming I researched during my training as a certified Life and Executive Coach. This can be a really transformational exercise if you visualize it. The illustration is we're going on a hot air balloon ride, which is an exhilarating experience I recommend you try at least once. Put that on the bucket list.

Imagine you're in a hot air balloon and as you slowly rise, gas is released into the burners with each tug of the rope. However, once you get to about seventy-five feet, you notice there's a rope keeping you tethered to the ground. As long as this rope is attached to the balloon, you actually feel a little safer because even though you're up pretty high, it's not so high you couldn't quickly return to earth with a few pulls from the ground crew.

The world you know is just below you and you're still very attached to that world. You can see the people you love on the ground cheering for you, happy you've gotten this far. The pilot hands you the rope and says to just give it a small tug, then off you go. You think about it for a moment, close your eyes, and tug. The rope spirals down to the ground and you watch your world moving further and further away from you.

As you climb further up, that sinking feeling wells up in the top of your stomach. It seems as if you're going to keep cruising right into outer space, never to see the people and things you care about again; but you know that's not true, even if it certainly feels like it.

Once you relax a little, you start to notice the balloon has stopped rising. You become more aware of your surroundings and begin to take in how beautiful everything is and how free you feel. The excitement turns to joy and you realize this joy must be what makes birds sing. You're flying and you're free; it's a wonderful feeling.

When you gave the rope a tug and watched it spiral down to the ground it was scary, and you thought maybe you made the wrong decision to take this ride. However just on the other side of letting go of that rope was freedom leading to unmanageable joy.

That rope is fear, and in order to master your message and find your voice you have to be willing to let go of the ropes in your life that are holding you back. Throw the rope over the side of the balloon and let it spiral down to earth. When fear tries to keep you grounded, let go of that rope. That's how you begin to understand and embrace your fear, which will ultimately lead to your being able to find your voice and master your message.

Sometimes You Have to Stand and Face Your Fear Head On

That's what my mother told me to do in so many words one hot summer day. Well, she actually told the five kids who were chasing me down the alley that I would fight them all one by one. These kids were the neighborhood Hurt Doctors, and that day they were making their rounds and I just happened to be their next patient.

My mother was on the back porch, probably hanging sheets out to dry, as Southern women do. I came bolting down the alley and jumped over the fence as the Hurt Doctors chased me. They froze in their tracks when they saw her standing there.

I thought, *Whew! Safe!* as if I had just slid into home plate, when she yelled, "Hey! What are you doing?" *At first I thought she was yelling at the kids chasing me, but then I realized she wasn't yelling at them; she was yelling at me.* I stopped dead in my tracks, stunned.

Just as they were about to take off running the other way she yelled to them, "Oh no, he's going to fight you all! But not at the same time! He's going to beat the crap outta of each one of you one by one!"

I looked at them first, then turned to her in what felt like slow motion, the look of horror on my face. She then turned to me in what was one of the calmest voices I'd ever heard and said, "Turn around and get to it, and you better not lose or you will have to deal with me."

I wasn't sure what to do, but I knew this much. When Dorothy Lee Sallie Beatrice Ross got quiet you better do whatever she said, so I turned around toward the Hurt Doctor gang and asked, "Who's first?" As I walked toward them, the looks that began to form on their faces were ones of confusion turned to the fear that this kid they were just chasing was now turning around and facing them.

Not only was I standing my ground, but I was walking toward them. As I moved forward they moved back, so I moved forward, faster, and my fear of what would happen when I got to them became less and less with each step. With every inch I gained a little more confidence. Just as I approached within a quick bound and hop of the fence they took off running down the alley and to my surprise I almost started chasing them.

Needless to say I was shocked. I turned back around walking back toward the house looking at my mother looking at me. I can't quote her because I don't recall everything she said but she did tell something I'll never forget.

Once you start running they'll never let you stop

Then the rest was something like most of the time if you stand tall to people and show them you're not afraid they will usually back down.

If they don't back down, you have to fight. Sometimes, even if you lose, you gain their respect because you faced them. However, I will only tolerate you fighting to defend yourself.

Even when I did have to fight, which was a lot in my neighborhood, I never had to fight that person again, I didn't lose much, and I never held a grudge.

Here's what I learned. If you do the unexpected, even a bad situation can be changed if you take control of it. I remember being terrified when I turned around, but thought, "If I can say something that will scare these dudes they may not put up much of a fight." My words, *Who's first,* made my actions even more provocative.

Here's something else I learned. You need to be able to quickly talk your way out of a situation because you can't fight everyone, and you won't always be able to scare off the people who are chasing you down.

I later refined and learned more about doing the unexpected to change outcomes post-high school, and after listening to *Personal Power* by Tony Robbins on audio tape. The lesson I recall was specifically about pattern interruptions, which is just the process of doing something unexpected in the midst of a situation to take the person's focus off the situation to something novel.

Framing

I've learned that when you enter a room, especially in meetings, to stop in the doorway and pause until everyone in the room takes notice of you, then proceed to walk in. This short pause frames you to the room like a picture frame, presenting you to them and making an unspoken impression of confidence which, especially if you're presenting, will make things go much more in your favor.

All this is before you've even spoken a word to the room. I started doing this in job interviews, at networking events, and any chance I could. Watch for this technique in movies.

In particular, I've seen it in James Bond movies with Sean Connery and others who played the title character. Notice how Bond enters a room and the confidence he exudes. I borrowed that same posture until I developed my own.

I've borrowed the best of what I've seen in other people in order to figure out what worked best for me. I'm of the opinion that you should think more of the person you would like to be, and then be that person. I'm not encouraging you to totally imitate someone else, but find the traits that get the results you want and make them a part of how you communicate with the rest of the world.

Do be careful not to be too much like any one person as you can lose yourself and find that you've become a persona that's not really true to who you are. I want to stress that when I study people like George Clooney, Brad Pitt, and Denzel Washington, both on screen and off, I'm looking for things I recognize in myself and working on those things to present a better me.

Top Three Ways to Deal with Fear

Here are my top three ways to deal with fear in just about any situation.

1. Give full acknowledgment that you're terrified. Yes, you have to acknowledge a feeling to deal with it

effectively, and fear is no exception. I use the following phrase. "Ok, this is scary and I'm really afraid, but what am I afraid of?" Then I take a mental inventory of those things and address each one.

2. Embrace the feeling. I embrace the feeling and notice everything about it, such as my breathing, or if I'm sweating or shaking. I notice what's going on around me and say, "Yes! I'm about to crush it."

3. Take *massive action*. This last step is the most important one.

Fear is the father of regret. If you don't take action you will never know what would have happened if you had. You have to take risks and live with no regrets about the things you never attempted, or the conversations you never had, or the people you were too afraid to speak to. If you look hard enough and talk long enough, you can talk yourself out of everything.

I want you to use fear as a gauge to talk yourself into everything. Of course you're not going to do absolutely everything and I'm not speaking of anything immoral. I'm speaking of the things we tell ourselves we can't do. Like speaking in front of an audience or starting a conversation at an event with a stranger.

Take action on these things and they will help you learn to master your message.

Chapter 4

THE SIRENS OF SHINY THINGS

On a call today, my book coach Morgan said something that was funny and ultimately became the title of this chapter. We were talking about things that distract us from our work of writing, and, of course, Shiny Object Syndrome came up, but she put it in a way I've never heard before.

I was talking about the hero's journey and how I wanted to build that type of story into this work. I was struggling to get the words down on paper and meet my writing goals. She said, "Yes, Vernon, I love the hero's journey you're on, but don't feel like you have to go on this long epic journey fighting sirens and such," and that's when I realized I had the title to this chapter and my writer's block disappeared, at least for the moment.

The Sirens of Shiny Things are real and they lure fledgling, and even experienced, entrepreneurs toward the craggy and shiny rocks of despair. For instance, a new software that's only $9.95 with a $37.00 upsell seems like a bargain; after all it's going to be something I'm going to use when I implement this new thing in my business, right?

Have you had that conversation with yourself before? I know I have all too often. Here's a screen shot of software, courses, and digital products I've purchased over the last year, and this is just a few.

Social Engage Purchased 02/09/2015 10:50 AM By: Precious Ngwu	VIEW DETAILS	**MemberDeliver - Pro Pack 15 Membership Courses - Launch Discount** Purchased 02/05/2015 11:20 PM By: Steve Benn	VIEW DETAILS
Friends of Justin Personal Success Program Pre-Launch Purchased 01/19/2015 1:14 PM By: Tiffany Lambert	VIEW DETAILS	**Optin Designer** Purchased 01/06/2015 1:37 AM By: Martin Crumlish	VIEW DETAILS
T-Shirt Titan Purchased 11/20/2014 12:26 AM By: Memeplex Limited	VIEW DETAILS	**Launch Has Closed Down** Purchased 11/03/2014 1:48 AM By: Sam Bakker	VIEW DETAILS
Launch Has Closed Down Purchased 11/02/2014 11:51 PM By: Sam Bakker	VIEW DETAILS	**SqueezeMatic** Purchased 08/09/2014 0:48 PM By: Brett Rutecky	VIEW DETAILS
Video marketing Business in a Box Upsell Purchased 07/31/2014 3:44 PM By: Dr. Amit Pareek (Sagius Limited)	VIEW DETAILS	**Video Marketing Biz in a Box Monster PLR** Purchased 07/31/2014 2:57 PM By: Dr. Amit Pareek (Sagius Limited)	VIEW DETAILS
OptinTango Purchased 06/14/2014 2:21 PM By: Leah Butler-Smith	VIEW DETAILS	**VideoMakerFX - Video Creation Software** Purchased 05/30/2014 7:30 AM By: Peter Roszak	VIEW DETAILS

I purchased a particular Wordpress theme with every intention of installing it over a weekend to upgrade the look of my website. Before I knew it, six weeks had passed and when I finally did install it I couldn't figure out how to get it set up, even with my extensive technical background.

I actually had to open a support ticket to remember where the support site was for this theme so I could remember what it looked like. If you're not laughing right now you should be because it's pretty funny.

It's the promise of not easy money, but easier money. It's not get rich quick; it's get a little richer slowly as you enhance what you're already doing.

These shiny things lure you toward the rocks of distraction with their songs of client-getting solutions, similar to how the Sirens of Greek Mythology would lure unsuspecting sailors to their demise.

Their beauty and angelic songs are intoxicating promises of effortless leads and more customers than you can handle. So many that you're going to need that new virtual assistant you've been thinking about anyway to free up your time, but somehow that never seems to happen in the thirty minutes they promised it would take for you to get going.

Time passes and you don't implement, or maybe you do but the effort is lackluster and so are your results, and once again your ship has run aground. You spend days or even weeks trying to implement this new thing but all that happens is you end up taking time away from what you intended on doing and now you're back at square one.

There are no new customers, but you've got a ton of tweets and Facebook posts that never really equaled new customers since you never got to your real goal of actually creating something of value because you were sucked into the Sirens of Shiny Things.

There is a Hero Here

Keep your faith, hero, because there's hope!

Remember, there's always hope, and your failures are stepping stones to success, but only if you continue forward down the path. Too often we take our failures and build paths that take us right back to the sirens. They lure us back to our old habits and keep us trapped in a never ending cycle of despair.

Failures are meant to be left behind us like stepping stones on a path. As you walk down the path you go from one stone to the next, and even if you stumble on the edge of one stone you keep walking. Imagine you're actually building the path you're going down as you lay each new stone in front of you, one by one.

Every stone you lay is going to be different than the last, but the key is to keep moving forward away from the Sirens of Shiny Things.

They will never stop calling to you because it's what they do and it's their purpose, and you *will* want to return to them. Sometimes you'll turn around to see them closer than you imagined, but looking down you can see the stones you've laid and your past failures that lead back to the sirens, but in front of you is new ground waiting on you to place the next stone of success. *Remember, your message moves you forward.*

Chapter 5

HOLDING ON TO YOUR DREAMS

CHASING BALLOONS

I t's amazing when you realize how much power you give away by not going after your dreams. You don't know it at the time, but when you settle for things being just ok, you're slowly giving away small parts of your power, and usually to things that aren't important to you. After all, it's what we are conditioned to do, isn't it?

Think about it. You mention something to a friend or family member what you're interested in doing, and if it's just a little outside of their comfort zone you might hear this response: "Oh, I don't know if that's a good idea." Notice I mentioned *outside of their comfort zone*, not yours.

You've already given thought to this new idea, but still you seek approval and validation from the people you're closest to. Wanting to do things outside of your comfort zone means you're growing. Growth means change, and change can be painful for others. New is exciting, but it also means there could be a significant risk. Risk isn't something most people feel comfortable taking, especially if they don't see themselves growing with you. They may try to slow you down, and not because they don't want the best for you, but because they want to protect you from disappointment.

Remember when you were a kid and lost your first balloon? I hope you've had this experience and if not, put this down and go buy a balloon and tie a twenty dollar bill to the string. Then let it go and you will understand the kind of pain I'm talking about.

Think back to when you actually lost that balloon. Either the wind caught it or you actually opened your hand and let it go, thinking you could catch it but instead it blew away. You chased it, but you weren't quick enough to grab it back.

No matter how hard you ran, your little legs couldn't help you catch up to that balloon. Your parents may have tried to help you, but they could only do so much.

Now imagine the balloon is your dreams and they keep blowing away because you aren't holding on tight enough. And the strong winds make it even worse. They constantly blow and rip your balloon away from you as you watch it drift further and further away. And there's nothing you can do, and from time to time you catch it but then another wind comes along. Maybe your parents or friends tell you to give up because you can't reach high enough to catch it or that you're not fast enough.

Constantly the winds are blowing against you and stealing the balloons of your dreams, but really the only one that's allowing your balloon to get away is you. The wind is the wind and it's doing what it's supposed to do, it's blowing.

By mastering your message and finding your voice, you gain the strength to hold on to your dreams and keep your balloons close to you, and with time your message can help others hold onto their balloons as well, or even give them new balloons to hold on to.

Holding on to your dreams by understanding your message is powerful and will deliver you. I promise.

Chapter 6

I CAN'T STAND HOW I SOUND

A man is what he thinks about all day long.
—**Ralph Waldo Emerson**

This is a pretty common thing I hear from podcasters and almost anyone who has to listen to themselves on audio or video. Many times I think we've all heard celebrities say they've either never seen one of their own films or they hate the way they look on camera. I think it's so common for people to be too critical of how they appear to others that it was not surprise to me when I heard, "Dad, I can't stand my voice."

Christina, my oldest girl, is away in college and taking classes for her major in Digital Media Production. During our

43

conversation, Tina was telling me about one of her classes and the latest assignment, which was to make a recording with a group. As we reviewed the details of the assignment and talked about editing, Christina exclaimed, "But Dad, I can't stand my voice!" It sounded very familiar, especially since I've said those very words about myself.

After we talked for a while, reviewing the audio, she went on to say, "I know what it is; I'm just trying to find my voice. I just haven't found it yet." Sidebar: I would totally be lying if I didn't share that I was extremely proud of my very self-aware twenty-something understanding that on her own.

The only thing I needed to do at this point was to help her understand that she was further along than she realized and that her internal conversation was causing doubt and preventing her from reaching her full potential and being comfortable with her voice.

The following steps are what I walked Christina through to find her voice.

Three Steps to Accepting Your Voice

1. **Get your mind right! Having the right mindset is the most important part of mastering your message.**

   It's a natural first step, a major key to understanding how you're currently viewing yourself, taking inventory of that perception, and owning it.

If you focus on how much you don't like your voice and that you sound horrible in front of people, then you probably will sound horrible. Like it or not, each person's perception of their reality is, in fact, their reality. You are what you believe.

How you feel on the inside comes out through your voice, whether you're talking to a group of people or just one person sitting across from you. Even through a microphone, how you're feeling comes out.

Something I would often do is ask someone I knew who attended the speaking gig or event, "Did I sound okay? I didn't sound stupid or unintelligent, did I?" Yes, I would ask those questions, but even as I'm writing this I wonder how it was I could have ever thought that way. I believe we all go through that stage.

So, anytime you're getting ready to speak, clear your mind of everything negative you think and instead say something like, "This is going to be so much fun! I love talking to people and learning what they have to say." Even in a meeting with people you talk to every day, start by saying you're excited to give the upcoming update.

Of course, smiling and excitement isn't for every situation, but for the purpose of this discussion I just want you to focus on loving the way you sound, and getting excited about your subject or topic really helps to move your focus from how you sound to how much you enjoy what you're saying and the impact it can have.

2. **Do your research and know your material.**

Always, and I mean always, start by taking the time to dig into the details of whatever you're talking about.

For example, I think there's nothing worse than talking to a podcaster who's invited you on their show, only to ask the host to introduce yourself to their audience. If this is you then stop it!

It only takes five solid minutes of research to read a bio and commit some of it to memory. I received some great advice from Chris Cerrone, a fellow podcaster and a dear friend. We were talking about podcasting and intros for the guest, when I said that I recorded them after the interview so I could get them down perfectly. Chris replied with something like this, "Why would you do that? Think about it this way, V; people love to hear about themselves. I think it really warms up the guest and gets them in interview mode. It gets you excited and makes them more willing to share."

What great advice! I started doing what he recommended and almost every time I am thanked for my wonderful introduction. I think it shows special interest in that person and that you care enough about them to know their stuff. It goes from just being an interview to an experience and your guest feels more valued. These people become amazing resources and could even become good friends.

3. **You have to start.**

One of the most difficult things people have problems with is starting because they so dreadfully hate the sound of their own voice.

One of the things that helped me become comfortable behind the microphone is actually having to listen back to my voice when editing a podcast or listening back to a talk I've given. Something I do to become more comfortable with the microphone, or the camera for that matter, is I picture myself having a conversation with the microphone or camera.

Read this Next Section Aloud

I'm actually having a conversation with this microphone in front of me. It's my tool, just as if I had a pen in my hand and were drawing a beautiful picture. My voice is the pen and I'm drawing this stunning landscape for my audience.

If I'm too self-conscious about the way I sound, I'm not using the tool to the best of its ability. I'm not serving my audience. But with this tool I can craft my words to elicit feelings in my audience to express exactly how I'm feeling and connect with how each person in the audience is feeling.

However, that will never happen if you don't start.

Read this Next Sentence Aloud

I'm willing to sit down and get to work if I want any of this to happen.

You have to practice consistently to become comfortable with hearing your voice and the more it becomes a part of who you are. The more you practice, the more your sessions become a performance; and when you're performing with that level of comfort, you're using your voice to help other people. When you think about your voice in that way you'll start to love how your voice sounds and you will want to talk to people and express yourself even more. There's divine beauty in understanding how your voice can change a person's mood or even change their life.

Your voice is a gift and I want you to master it.

Chapter 7

WHY I RESISTED THE NICHE

N iche down until it hurts." I've heard this said before and it's in direct contradiction to everything I actually believe in. The thought of working on or being known for just one thing bothers me.

Here's why.

When I was growing up, and perhaps other African Americans of a certain age will identify with this, my mother would say to me, "You're black, and unfortunately that means you have to work twice as hard to go half as far as the white person sitting right next to you." She also explained that was no reason to complain or hold resentment in my heart toward white folks. Some people are good and some are not, but either way she said, "You have to work hard for whatever you want, and you have to be the best."

My sister and I would hear this all the time, sometimes daily. Unfortunately, I heard it more because at the time I was a total screw up. I digress. Let's get back to niching down.

In my life I've had to be good at everything I've done to even be considered. Let me explain that statement a little.

When I was a busboy, I was the best and got the most tips because I worked harder than anyone else. I was moved up to waiting tables because I worked harder and did more than anyone else at various places. When I worked at the Sharper Image, I started in the stockroom and in order to get on the sales floor I had to be able to explain every item in the store to the store manager before he would let me sell. So I did, and after about twenty minutes of doing demonstrations I was promoted and from then on was always in the top two in sales.

In the IT field, if I were asked to do something, I've always had to be able to do it, and if I didn't know it I needed to learn it quickly and execute it perfectly. I've always felt if I didn't know how to do something I would either not be considered for the next thing or I would lose my job. I've been presented that option too, so it wasn't just in my head. Mistakes, no matter how small, have always impacted my career more than those of my counterparts.

So, in business as a solopreneur, I've also adopted the I-must-do-everything-on-my-own attitude, and to be honest, I've done it exceptionally well.

It shouldn't come as a surprise that often delivering our messages is much like the way we run our businesses. It's all over the place with no real focus. Niching down to one thing has always felt like I'm limiting myself and missing out on opportunity.

Why not speak to everyone about anything they ask me to speak on? Speak to kids about motivation, sales teams about B2B selling, or anything that's interesting. That's what I prefer to do. And even though it's not my target audience, I'll be able to tailor something to them. After all, I can make $1,200 for a forty-five-minute talk. I consider that a win!

The problem is I was putting profit over my message and over principle. Now, I didn't take the job talking to kids about motivation, but came real close to taking it because it's hard to walk away from that kind of money. I also feel like I could have pulled it off given my past academic record, but really it just didn't fit.

It's like when I was doing web programming after reading a few magazines, a couple of books, and attending a few classes. I was ready to start making money as a web programmer and building websites. But ultimately building websites wasn't what I wanted to do, so even though I made some money in that area, there wasn't very much satisfaction after the project was finished.

The point is that when you're trying to find your voice, you have to focus on one message. Even if it's a one-on-one conversation, you have to be focused on the point of that conversation and what you're trying to communicate.

Not understanding what you stand for or what's important to you in a conversation generally leads to confusion, or at least it won't be a productive exchange of ideas. You might hear this on a podcast here or there that seems to ask random questions that don't really lead the guest down a path that makes any definable sense except to the podcaster.

Being intentional is what helped me refine my message and become focused on what I wanted to talk about and who I wanted to talk to.

Chapter 8

INTENTIONAL CONVERSATIONS

It usually takes me more than three weeks to prepare a good impromptu speech.

—Mark Twain

I recently read the book *Intentional Living* by John C. Maxwell. I definitely recommend you check it out. It's an easy read, but even if you're like me, you can just grab the audiobook and listen to it over the course of a couple of days. In this book, Maxwell discusses living and approaching life with an actual plan for what you want to achieve.

Earlier I talked about not really having a plan defined for my life. I knew I wanted to take care of my family and to not be poor. I recall going on a class field trip to IBM around fourth or fifth grade and telling myself I would one day work there. I had no idea what power that intention would have.

I found out about twenty years later, actually, when I found myself working at IBM in a job I loved. The only problem was I didn't have a plan for what to do next. I was able to get to that position based on how I could relate to people and the ability to pick up on technology, not necessarily on my skill set.

I truly believe that when you're communicating and in the process of mastering your message, you must absolutely be intentional in what you plan on saying. Even in your random conversations, you must be intentional. I'm not talking about pretending you're really engaged, but *actually* being engaged in every conversation and listening with the intent of contributing real value to the conversation.

If you listen with intention and the hope of learning and contributing, I truly believe whatever your message is at the time you will achieve mastery of it.

What does intentional conversation really mean? For me, it means giving full attention to every conversation. My wife will read that last sentence and be like, *Hold up*. Don't be mad, sweetheart; I'm not perfect. What I'm talking about is how often when we're talking, I'll try multitasking by looking at email or replying to a text or Snapchat message thinking I'm paying attention to her. It's a bad habit and I'm better than I used to be, but it still does happen even though I'm telling you not to do it. You won't be perfect at being intentional in your conversations, but it's worth continuing to attempt to master it.

How to Give Your Full Attention

Here's a tip for giving your full attention when having a conversation. If you're in the middle of a conversation and feel the need to look down at your phone, or you *do* look down and then realize what you just did, say, "I'm sorry; my intention was to give you my full attention. Let me put this away." Then put the dang phone in your pocket. Most likely the person will give you a pass since you acknowledged them, and I'd wager your actions probably made them feel as though they were important enough to deserve your full attention. You'd be surprised how far that goes in today's world.

Like I mentioned before, I'm pretty bad when it comes to the phone and conversations with my family, which honestly are the conversations and interactions that count the most. This might explain why we all seem to be so bad at it.

I'm sure you've heard the old saying about how we hurt the ones closest to us. It's true, and it's still a struggle for me to not get distracted with other things. I think the acknowledgment of it and actions toward changing those behaviors helps move me closer to always improving my communication and ultimately helps me master my message with family. *I'm a total work in progress.*

Chapter 9

MASTERING YOUR MESSAGE ON SOCIAL MEDIA

O f course, I have to write a chapter dedicated to social media. There are so many misconceptions about engagement and what works on the Internet. There's no shortage of advice on how to, what to, and when to post, tweet, snap, wav, and just about everything else. It's no wonder so many business owners, journalists, and digital marketers (agencies especially) have so many issues with getting the messaging right to fit their audience.

There's no way for me to go into each network with a case study and the best methods for each. That's another book entirely that Gary Vaynerchuck wrote a couple of years ago called *Jab, Jab, Jab, Right Hook*.

What I am going to give you is my take on what I've found to be effective, and in general what my best practices are in regard to finding your voice on social media; this might be a slightly different take on what you're used to hearing.

Start with What You Hate

I've never actually liked Facebook.

I'm sure my friends won't be shocked to read this. If we've ever had a conversation about social media you've heard me either say that I hate Facebook and Myspace is king (I'm not kidding), or that it's not my main network when I'm being nice.

However, you really can't ignore Facebook any more than you can ignore Google for search. I like to call it a necessary— and I won't go so far as to say *evil*—but it *must* be a part your activity on social.

What I've learned about the various social networks is they each have a certain cadence to them. Each has a rhythm and a method for how the real influencers of the platform communicate most effectively. You should learn to understand what that cadence is and use it to establish a truly responsive audience.

Facebook is a very strange mix of personal and business, and that doesn't always translate to how you began your journey on the platform, which I think is what causes so many problems for so many people. In my case, I joined Facebook as an adult. As of this writing, I've been on Facebook for nine years! However, when I joined Facebook I wasn't doing anything with social media, marketing, or coaching. Since then my audience has changed based on who I am now and what my interests currently are, and so has the way in which I communicate with that audience. That recognition is key to finding your voice for your current situation.

The cadence on social media is how the conversations flow, and what's expected and accepted based on the relationship you've developed with your audience. For instance, I think it's totally out of line to just start talking about business when the network you've established on a platform is full of people who aren't interested in talking about business. If you pay attention to what your audience is posting, liking, and sharing, you'll know if they can bear to deal with your constant business posts.

I have well over a thousand friends and growing on Facebook with whom I've established a personal network. As my business and interests have evolved, I've learned to ease my audience into the type of conversations I want to have and let them know I would be posting more business and coaching related updates and they could decide if they want to read them or not.

Once, when I mentioned my frustration with the lack of engagement from my audience for business-related posts, but how I got hundreds of "likes" and comments for updating my photo with a family picture, my best friend since the age of fifteen, Brian Wallace, said something to me that has been a guiding light in how I communicate now on social media.

Brian said, "Dude, when you post that business stuff it's too much like work, so I really just scroll past it." He continued to say, "Now, when you post family stuff or something that's funny, that's what I get on Facebook for." That was a lightbulb moment for me. I realized I was delivering the right message to the wrong audience. No wonder the pic of me and the kids and my nephew got dozens of comments and hundreds of likes, but a post about personal development and growth got two likes and no comments!

Brian, who's not even in the same industry as me, gave me the secret. *Give your audience what they want, not what you want or what you think they want, but actually what they want.*

You can give your audience business messages, but you better also be training them to recognize the difference so that you get the people in your audience who want that business message.

You can then get those people to engage with you on other platforms where they will be better served by your message. However, if you're trying to get that audience from Facebook, you can create a page or a group that will allow those people to follow you and engage outside of your normal social groups.

Side note. Keep in mind that on social media, the way you title a conversation, blog post, or the first few lines of a tweet can totally blow your chances of communicating the way you want and at the level of mastery you deserve. How you start the conversation is vital to mastery of your message.

I started with Facebook because it's not my favorite. I love Twitter and always will. I have the best engagement on that network and it's because I'm the most consistent there outside of LinkedIn.

For me, Twitter is what opens the door. I use Twitter to reach out, research, and make connections. Twitter can be a very effective tool for connecting on LinkedIn as well. If you're looking to make an outreach and start a conversation on LinkedIn or via email and know where a person is employed, Twitter works because most companies and influencers within companies often follow other people within the company, so it's easier to find out who's who.

Finding Your Voice on Social Media

I think everyone has their own opinion of the most effective use of social media, which tactics are most effective, and what automation you should use to appear to the person on the other end who you're interacting with.

That's one of the many things I think is wrong with social media—the desire to automate all of it away from one-on-one human interaction. I'm not sure how you're supposed to find your voice or your company's voice if the "bots" are the ones communicating with your customers. I think bots have their place in making some interactions effective, such as making a general announcement, but totally running your platform with them is not appropriate.

There aren't any secrets to finding your voice on social media, no matter the platform. I have a few guidelines I follow that help me to connect fully with the people I interact with online.

1. First, reach out to people I find interesting and that are doing things I admire.
2. Secondly, talk to those people about the things they're doing.
3. Lastly, I'm intentional in those conversations so that even if we never meet in person, they will feel like they know me based on talking with the people I connect with on a human level.

Chapter 10

MASTERS OF THEIR MESSAGE
How my Mentors and Friends Found Their Voices

PATRICE WASHINGTON
You Sound Horrible

I met Patrice Washington at the Financial Blogger's Conference in 2013. I was serving as a local media partner promoting the conference to the local bloggers and social media influencers.

At first I thought she was so down to earth. She was striking; I figured she was one of the speakers since she was so together. She was talking about the book she had just published and was selling in the FinCon Book Store that featured the attendees who had written books. I purchased a copy and had her sign it, and then later invited her to be a guest on my podcast.

Since then Patrice has gone on to become the only official co-host of the Social Strategy Podcast. She's been on three times, and anyone who's on that much deserves a spot anytime they want it.

Patrice has an amazing story of building a million-dollar business, only to lose it all in the real estate bust of 2008. Since then Patrice's wisdom on money matters has been featured by national brands such as NBC, *Black Enterprise*, *The Huffington Post*, *Upscale* magazine, and, most recently, as the personal finance voice of the top-rated and nationally syndicated *Steve Harvey Morning Radio Show*, on which she hosts her own weekly segment, *Real Money Answers with Patrice Washington*. In addition, she's made several appearances on the *Steve Harvey Show*.

In one particular interview, Patrice and I talked about how she first found her voice and how that experience has helped her to this day.

Vernon: When you were first starting out, like during your college days or when you started giving talks, how did you figure out what you wanted to say? How did you figure out what your personality was on stage?

Patrice: I figured it out through trial and error. Originally, I think of the subject matter and who I thought people wanted me to be. I thought I had to be super professional. I used to say, "I'm not a speaker," because I didn't consider myself as a motivational or a transformational speaker. I considered myself as a trainer, as I was typically training on a very specific topic. I was training on credit or on how to get your first home or how to budget successfully. I was training on very specific things, whereas now, I hardly do any of that unless it's my own course. Now, people just pay me to come and talk. There's a focus, but it's so much more about my story than it is about step 1: do this, step 2: do that.

I found my way just by starting, just by being the type of person who will go ahead and teach these three tips on this, these ten steps on that. Then I became more comfortable, which happened over time, and realized that even a chat with people after I would do those sessions, the thing that would stand out for them would always be something about a story I told.

I learned that I needed to illustrate points if I felt like I was losing people. So gradually, as a part of my speaking, I also became a storyteller, although that wasn't what I had set out to do. I just set out to talk about these ten steps, these ten points, these are the five ways, and then if I felt like I was losing people just by looking at the audience, I'd be like, "So you guys know when this happens and that happens? Okay, let me tell you a story…" Then I would realize what stuck with people more over time were the stories, not the ten steps and not the three ways of doing something.

It took a couple of years, though, for me to really recognize that because when I first started, I didn't set out to be a speaker. I was only there to show the information with the hopes of bringing them into real estate as clients. It wasn't to entertain anyone as a speaker. So it probably took a couple of years for me to realize all these points are great, but the only thing people remember are just stories. So I guess it was just starting and then paying attention to the audiences' feedback that helped me shift and grow as I have gone on.

Vernon: Have you ever gotten to the point where you would say, "You know what, I hate my voice?"

Patrice: In terms of my actual voice?

Vernon: Yeah, like how you sound in the microphone or how you sound during interviews. I know a lot of people actually go through that when they are trying to figure out what their voice is. I actually talk about it in one of the chapters of *Master Your Message*. People often have problems with not liking the way they sound.

Patrice: Wow, that's pretty interesting. I never had a problem with my voice, I guess because I have been hearing it for so long. I started speaking when my mom put me in the Easter pageants and in the Christmas plays so I was used to hearing myself.

I even used to hear playbacks from CDs, so it never really bothered me. In around 2010, we pitched to a radio station in Detroit to have me do a money segment where I had to record some Q&As and little money tips. We sent it to the Program Director of the station and his feedback to my husband was that my voice was hideous. That was the first time I had considered that there was something wrong with my voice. I had never even thought about it so that kind of hurt my feelings.

Vernon: Right! I would think it would, a little bit.

Patrice: I have been walking around for twenty-eight years with no idea that I sounded hideous.

Vernon: Right! Like I've been talking to people...I should not have been!

Patrice: I've been on my voicemails, I've been on my business and stuff, and I had no idea! And then after a couple of days, I thought, what did he mean? Maybe it was just strong and I started thinking about the people I knew—entertainers, people who considered had challenging voices—and thought that I don't sound anything like that. So I always tell people, I thought, so no one's going to give me a segment, I'm just going to create my own.

So the next year, my friend Clyde Anderson and I went on CNN hundreds of times as financial analysts. He and I got together and we started our own regular show, *Main street Radio*, we paid for it and all that, out in Atlanta on an AM station. We did that for a year and it got pretty popular. We did really well and built a good fan base and I never heard anyone say anything about my voice.

They might not agree with my opinion but my voice was not a problem, so I just took it that it was that guy's loss. You know how that works, he now has to listen to it every week on the *Steve Harvey Show*.

Vernon: Hahaha, right? Remember what you said? You could've had this in your station.

Patrice: Right. You could've been the one to help launch me, but you tell me my voice is hideous. It's crazy. But that was the only experience I ever had about my voice.

Vernon: That's interesting. So did you ever have the experience of the first time you really stepped on stage and realized, 'You know what, this is what I should be doing?'

Patrice: Absolutely. I can't say that it was when I was in the real estate business because my mind was just not there; I was not even thinking of becoming a speaker. I heard Von Franklin speak when I was a freshman in college and he was a senior at UST. He spoke during my freshman orientation and that was the first time that I was like, "Wow, that's cool. I want to do that one day. You could do that. Look at him; he's so young." It was a fleeting thought, but I got out of college and would do it to help promote my business but because it was very technical when I started, I didn't get a lot of joy out of it. I wasn't nervous; it was something I could do and I was marking how many people I could bring at the end of the talk to sign up for my services. That was my focus.

And then I started working at Operation Help in Atlanta. When I was teaching even just five people in the library, I was having such a good time. By then I learned to tell stories because I knew from the previous period to tell stories, bring people in, and to use props, so it became fun. Then I was like, "This is what I should be doing. This is all that I should be doing." And the people and my boss at that time—God rest his soul, he passed on 2014. He passed the night of my Win Conference in 2014—would tell me, "You don't belong here; you're above this." I would say, "I belong where the paycheck is" [laughs]. He would tell me all the time, "You are supposed to be talking to five thousand, not five people."

I had the opportunity when I was all over Atlanta to do these talks to five people or fifty people, sometimes a hundred fifty, maybe the most when I was there was three hundred people, but it was just preparation. It was my opportunity to perfect my stories, to get comfortable, really comfortable, on the stage, so it didn't matter how many people were there, I could still do whatever I needed to do. It was an opportunity to really perfect it but I realized working at Operation Help that that's what I was supposed to do, and that's when I started to pursue it and started getting booked for gigs. I wouldn't even say booked; I started to volunteer to do gigs outside of Operation Help because my goal was to speak somewhere every week and if we didn't have something on the books for Operation Help then I just went to a church or reached out to places and did it anyway because I just wanted to practice.

Vernon: That's awesome. I wasn't trying to make the book a book for speakers because there are a lot of things out there like that. I'm not trying to teach people how to give a speech or how to talk to a room full of people, although I think they'll get it from the book. It's more of, how do you figure out what your message is? How do you know what it is that you should be talking about or that you should be talking to people? It may not be just talking to people; it may be interviewing people. How do you find that voice and when you do, are you paying attention? Are you recognizing what you are being told?

The first time I talked to a group of people, it was many, many years ago when I was working for this company called Unicare and I had to do a presentation. It was the first time I did a PowerPoint presentation and it's still one of the best presentations I have given, and they were super impressed. And from that, I ended up working with them, helping them do some stuff like pitching hospitals and it went off from there. That was kind of it and then some other stuff here and there.

I was at a Microsoft conference, a small business conference in Chicago, and we were a preferred vendor for some Microsoft item that I was selling (I couldn't even remember what it was now) but it was me and a friend and he got up there and he was just nervous. We each had to get up there and had to introduce ourselves to the room and it was bad. So I said, "Let me get up there and save this dude because he is not like this." He didn't know he had to stand in front of anybody and talk. I didn't either but when I got up there it felt natural. I said, "This is cool," and it just went from there.

But the very, very first time, [I tell this story a little earlier in the book] I had to get in front of a group of people I didn't know, I was at a retreat. My priest had this retreat and there was a bunch of white kids, me and then this other black kid from our church. I was Catholic so it was a Catholic church. One of the altar boys and me (I wasn't an altar boy at that time because I would never show up on Sunday, at least not on time as I always wanted to come to the late service and come in late so I can never do the altar boy thing), it was the first time I had been away from home and there were like thirteen or fourteen white folks, my priest was there, and this other kid that I sort of got along with at school. We were supposed to be getting along and sharing things. I found it interesting… I have been around white people but in our city, most of the people I have been related to are just like me. There wasn't any racism, nothing I recognized, but I just felt like I just got to say what I need to say so they thought I was super shy.

It got to this point where he had to do a presentation, a play, like a skit. I don't know exactly how it happened but they elected me to be the spokesperson and we were supposed to do a game show. I was like, "This is not going to be good," but I have seen the movie *Risky Business* and there was a line in there where they were having a conversation where one of the guys says, *Sometimes you just have to say f--- it and go for it,* so I just went into this crazy rant and was imitating a character in *Bewitched* or some game show host that I have seen who was just all over the place and was loud and obnoxious.

They were all jaws opened to the ground because I was just all over the place and super full of energy. It felt right and all the while I was thinking, *Wow, this is interesting, this is super crazy.* Then this guy wrote me a letter a couple of weeks or months later just to see how I was doing and he said, "Man, you had everybody shocked; you just came out of nowhere. We all thought you were really, really shy." And I said, "Well, yeah, I was.…"

Patrice: I used to have dreams of being onstage when I was a kid, and when I try to tell people about the dream everyone thought that I wanted to be a model. I see the people, I'm onstage, but I'm not walking down the runway. It was in high school when I was elected class president and I used to have to get those unruly kids in order, give the announcements, and talk about what was coming up and the money we needed to raise. I had a homeroom teacher, Mr. Butner, who also passed away, who everyone hated back in the day. People got offended by what he was saying and I loved it. I was his pet even the first day I came into his homeroom. I gave him hell but we understood each other's crazy. Mr. Butner told me, the way you command the attention of these kids is amazing. And he told me this when I was in tenth grade.

I never thought about that until right now until we had this conversation but I have seen myself on the stage, in the auditorium, at the school that I went to from fifth to twelfth grade and, without being nasty, how I used to get people to pay attention. When you think about it and you go as far as you can, I think there have been signs along the way. I'm still nervous when I tape television or if I get up to speak; it's not as if the butterflies leave, but I'm also not that afraid. My knees are not buckling, I don't vomit before I start…that's the reality with some people, those are the extremes. Yeah, you made me think of Mr. Butner, which is so cool. I remember just laughing but he was actually speaking something into my life that I didn't fully recognize until 2011. 2011 was when I thought that I should do this for a living.

Vernon: How did you make that transition?

Patrice: To doing it for a living?

Vernon: Yeah.

Patrice: When I got to Atlanta, I didn't really know anyone except for my brother and a few other people. I knew I was supposed to teach Financial Education so I wanted to find a way to dig deeper into it so I signed up to volunteer. Everywhere that I volunteered to speak, before they hired me on as a full-time employee, and even when I was employed, people would tell me. For me, transition was more like I knew it was coming but I wasn't hard-pressed to do it, if that makes sense…

Vernon: It does. You just take natural steps to get into it.

Patrice: Yeah, I knew it was coming but unlike some people who are so desperate to be this world-class speaker, I felt like it's going to come naturally as long as I do what I'm supposed to do. And at this point what I'm supposed to do is perfect my story. I'm supposed to perfect my timing because I had a big problem with going over time when I first started. Give me an hour, it's going to be an hour and fifteen, give me thirty and it's going to be forty. And I realized that if you want to do this as a profession, you should respect the time that's given to you. I felt that innately but I wasn't good at it yet. But I don't want to be one of those people where you got things really good but since you're on your fifty-eighth minute, you would say, "I have more for you but because of the time, I'm going to stop now. I'm not going to keep going." That's rude to the audience. I didn't want to be one of those people so the only thing I could think of was to keep my stories succinct or learn how to transition. You can keep your story down from twenty minutes to three minutes and still make your point. I felt that during that time, I'm just supposed to practice that.

What started happening was that people started asking me, so in addition to Operation Help, the weeks that I wasn't speaking there, I would meet people and agree to come to their church during the weekend. Sometimes it was a free event, sometimes it was paid. I was charging $250 to talk and sometimes it'd be like, "That's okay, I just wanted to talk anyway." Some people will say, "Our budget is only $500," and I would say, "Okay, I can work with that." So I transitioned because people forced me to transition. The transition happened because I was willing to put the time in and perfect what I was doing. For me it wasn't, "I'm going to do twenty-five speeches to practice and then just go and start charging $5,000 to talk. That wasn't my plan. I just wanted to keep perfecting where I am at the moment, and then the market basically taught me to keep moving forward. I wouldn't have charged anyone $15,000 to talk, until someone says we got $15,000 for you and I'd say, "Okay, yeah, that's about my fee." [laughs]

Vernon: I love that; that's funny!

Patrice: So every step of the way, I always talk about that everything for me was very spirit-led. So yeah, I'm a planner, of course I set my goals, and just to protect the integrity of the brand, there are things that I won't do or gigs that I won't take obviously, but every step of the way, in terms of my growth, it's really been all about paying attention to the cues from the marketplace. I don't think I had the uphill battle that a lot of people had because I'm not fighting anything. There's no resistance; I'm not trying to get this and have the marketplace tell me I'm only worth that. Does that make sense?

Vernon: It makes perfect sense because so many speakers try to go for the, "I'm only going to do $1,500 talks or between $1,000 - $1,500 or $2,000 - $5,000. I won't take anything other than that." And then they would say, "I'm not sure if your budget meets my fees or this is my hotel cost, this is my travel cost…" They try to make it too much of a business and they try to worry about, "I have to book the gig," instead of what value they are going to offer and if talking to people more important than getting paid to talk to the people.

Patrice: Yes, that's it right there. That is such a great line. I really believe that when you focus on the people and whatever you are called to talk about or train on, it'll all come together. Yes, you have to be a business person and you don't want to be taken advantage of, but in the same respect, you don't want to play yourself either and burn bridges before you can get there.

There's a girl who's conference I'm going to speak at; she's been trying to book me for the last couple of years. It's more about timing, but every time she comes back from her conference the following year, my fee has gone up and she can't afford me. And this year, she reached out and booked me and she was so excited that she got $5,000 today. But we told her, "Ah, we are at $8,500," and then I said, "No, we just have to do it because she had been loyal, she comes back every year. She started at $2,000, $3,500, $5,000 and it's not her fault." Just out of respect for her and out of respect for the people. I have to value my time but I am most concerned about being able to do what I love. It's a business but it's also a heart thing. Can you get me to fly across the country for $2.00? No, unless you are part of my free giveaways for the year, probably not. But I do try to work with people as well. I think where a lot of people miss the mark, especially when first starting out or growing to the next level, is trying to be complicated and trying to be bigger than you probably are. It's always interesting to me how people will say, "You are the best and nicest person to work with," then they tell me horror stories and I will reply, "She was rude to you, how? Tell me again what she got going on because

I'm confused." The reality is, no matter what you have going on, you shouldn't be a douche bag.

Vernon: Exactly. That is a line right there.

Patrice: No matter what you have going on, don't be a douche bag. You should still be respectful because things are cyclical. You are going to have some down times in your business and you are going to wish those people will hire you at whatever rates those are.

I'm trying to do things virtually, and if you look at my office right now, I am in the process of taking things paperless. Streamline my life to live between cities and doing this stuff in preparation for the fact that I do want to have another child. When I told my husband I'm gracious to people, it's because I can go on hiatus. Beyond an online presence, you won't hear anything from me. If I have a child, I'm going to be a ghost. Besides a tweet and a social media update, you are not going to see me flying anywhere and doing all this stuff. Coming out of that, I am always gracious to people because I might need that $2,500 check when I'm ready to get back on the road. I might have to feel my way back up and I'm totally aware of that being a possibility and I am okay with that. I think when people miss it is when they get their ego in the way and you just start thinking that you are more than you are. It's not saying that you shouldn't have confidence, but don't be arrogant.

Vernon: Yeah, all of it comes with a price. You don't have to play the games, so to speak. At least not that game. I remember you saying that you were willing to talk to three or more who gather…

Patrice: Yeah, that's the truth. If I would meet people when I was out and about, even if it's for Operation Help, and someone would come up to me and say, 'Oh, I wish my sisters were here," I would say, "Put your sisters together and I'll come to your house." I used to do in-home things because I just wanted to talk. Back to your point, if that's truly your calling, you're going to do it regardless. By the fact that you are doing it regardless, you are going to perfect it and the dollars that you want will come in.

When I look at people like ET, Earl Thomas, he is getting $50,000-$75,000 a talk; but before he was getting that he was just out talking. Remember, he is a pastor so he just talks anyway. It probably sounds cliché but, especially if you are just getting started or moving to the next level, it just can't be all about the money. I think you miss the mark when that's all you focus on. It's such a distraction. You got to survive but that's why this is something that you should build alongside something else. I don't know how a person just becomes a speaker…like I'm going to quit my job and be a speaker.

Vernon: Right. It should be complimentary to a business or something else that you do.

Patrice: Exactly. Like if I only was a speaker, there might be months that I wouldn't eat. There are months when I do three or four things really well, but there are months when I don't really do anything in terms of speaking. So offer other products or services like coaching, consulting, or other things. Maybe it's just me; maybe I need to do more, but I'm happy with what I'm doing.

Vernon: No, don't change that. That seems to be one of your strengths; you do, what you're happiest doing. It sets you apart from other people. I don't think I've seen you do anything that seems unnatural, which is one of the reasons why I respect you so much.

Patrice: Even when we think about how we promote using Periscope and all these different platforms or whatever, I hear people say all the time, "You should do this, you should do that." I'm open to learning new things but I will only do what feels authentic to me because it becomes a burden and a job if I don't like what I'm doing anymore. And right now, I love what I do. I'm always looking to grow, to perfect systems and things like that but I'm only going to do what feels good for me. So if I endorse it, you know that it's real. You know that I truly believe in it. I'm not just going to do whatever just to get a dollar because money is not the first thing on my mind. It's part of the plan but it's not the first thing on my mind.

Patrice C. Washington is a three-time bestselling author and has been making money educational, yet fun, since 2003. She is a featured columnist, television commentator, radio host, keynote speaker, and leading authority on personal finance. She's also the financial voice of the *Steve Harvey Morning Show*. Learn more at *http://realmoneyanswers.com*.

CHRIS BROGAN

Using His Voice to Serve

I discovered Chris a long time ago when reading *Trust Agents* and never thought I would get the chance to meet him or become friends. I have to credit my connection to Chris with not being afraid to introduce myself and be myself. Our first meeting in real life was short but a great one. I saw him and said, "Hey Chris, it's great to meet you in person! I comment on your blog." He was gracious and that was it. I moved on and left him to deal with all the other fans who were trying to get his attention.

When meeting celebrities it's best to give them space. Show respect for their work and your admiration for them, then move on. They will remember the person that gave them space and not the people that crowded them. You can them follow up with them later on or after the event. It's part of knowing who you are and mastering your message.

Here's Chris's story as told by him.

My voice started somewhere around age five or six. My parents were (and are) very encouraging people. They convinced me that the world was mine, and I believed them. I told (really bad) jokes on stage at a daycare center talent show. I modeled clothes at a department store. I played in school band. For an introvert, being on stage was one of my favorite places.

Also around age five, I was convinced that I was meant to be an author. I started writing really bad stories for a while, then stopped. But I told everyone I was an author. It was one of my primary identities for years and years before I actually started earning it.

What goes into my voice? First, I talk to everyone the same way, whether I'm on stage or writing a book or sitting across from them in a coffee shop. I'd describe that voice as a mix of weird humor and heartfelt intentions of being helpful. I tend to use somewhat unique turns of phrase. I feel that too many of us use the "tried and true" and thus, never get the chance to stand out.

I can tell you that there's one real simple calculated part of my voice. I intend to connect. Every time I speak, I want to connect with the person who is giving me their attention.

When I spoke to an auditorium full of sixth graders, I talked about video games that I played and that they might play, and I talked about current YouTube stars before diving into my talk. They *knew* that I knew what they were into. That intention to connect runs through everything I do.

I had a teacher in one of the seven colleges I attended. His name was Ken Hadge and he was a businessman. I learned so much from Ken. One of his favorite and oft-repeated expressions was, "Tell it to me like I'm six years old." He hated big words. At the same time, I was obsessed with the book *The Shipping News*, by E. Annie Proulx. Her sentences were short. All of them. Like this. Sometimes not even sentences. Like. This.

That really informed my writing style. I know a lot of big words. I use almost none of them. I keep it to three syllables or less all the time. One reason is that I don't want people to feel intimidated (Dang, that was five syllables.). The other reason is that I want the ideas I'm sharing to be easy to absorb. And I know a secret about most people who use a lot of big words.

They're afraid. They're afraid that people will think they're not smart, not important, not "worth it." Big words are a great way to shout loudly that you're worried others won't take you seriously.

Sure there are exceptions. If you work around doctors and rocket scientists, it's okay to use bigger words. But most of us?

Talk more clearly, with simpler words, and fewer of them. The world will thank you for it.

I believe that every "unique" voice is informed from several sources and inspirations. We are the product of what we consume, right? I love motivational speakers and coaches. I love people like Tony Robbins (he interviewed me for his *Internet Money Masters* series), Stephen R. Covey, Les Brown, Harvey McKay, Tom Peters (we keynoted together at a conference once and he's so lovely), David Sedaris, and probably many more people who aren't immediately coming to mind.

The writers who informed my voice are varied. E. Annie Proulx, Chuck Palahniuk, Charles Bukowski, Henry Rollins, Tom Peters, Richard Branson, Dan John, James Altucher. What I've taken from all these people varies, but at the core, what is similar about them all is they all work to get to the heart of what they want to talk about, to the bare truth. They aren't afraid to upset and offend on the way to delivering something they feel is important that we know and understand.

That's really the core of great communication and voice, my friend. What you most need to know is this: it is always about them.

Your ability to create a powerful and unique voice has very little to do with who you are and what makes you wonderful and why you're a great and special snowflake. Everything that goes into making you who you are is just the instrument upon which you play a beautiful song for others.

You exist to serve.

If you miss this detail. If you skip over this, you'll miss it all and be one of those "sounds like everyone else" people. I can tell you that all the "never seemed to make it far" voices and speakers and people trying to be someone (emphasis on "trying to be") are all people who didn't realize that the most important ingredient of this whole cake is that we're here to serve others. We're here to use our voices to help others grow. Our job is to give other people skills and tools and knowledge and wisdom and heart.

No one cares about us. Well, someone does. But that's not why you decide to be a speaker or a writer or a voice in the world.

Voices in the world exist as beacons to guide others to where they're going. We rarely look at the beacon, except for guidance. But the beacon isn't the destination. It's a guide point.

That's our job.

But to shine like that requires polish. If you are mucked up in your own self, if your voice is messy with your own self-doubts and worries and lack of confidence, you can't be much of a beacon for others. If you're trying too hard to get attention for yourself, then what good are you in your job of helping others get where they need to go?

I'll tell you another story about me because it might become a story about you. Along the arc of my life, I went from being a weirdo that not many people paid attention to in any given day to being a weirdo that a lot of people gave their time and attention. I went from being picked last in gym class to being someone that others crowded around to get a photo with.

That messes with you. That fills you with a really poisonous ego problem. And it can ruin everything, if you let it.

It will come. It happens to everyone fortunate enough to develop a voice worth following. But it's your job to remember this and implement it all the time: accept neither praise nor criticism, as both are poison.

When someone says something nice to me, I thank them. When someone says something negative to me, I thank them. I always consider whether they're right in both cases. But I throw both praise and criticism away. I work from my own inner goals. To *not* do this is dangerous. To play to the love and appreciation of the crowd is a terrible thing, because what happens is that you end up going in circles, down wrong roads, and lose your ability to guide others toward bigger success.

To sum up everything I want to tell you in our brief time together, I'll resort to bullets.

- You exist to serve others and guide them toward greater success.
- Your voice should be the same onstage and off, and it comes from finding your own truth, whether or not that's anyone else's truth.
- To shine, you need to polish away your own self-interests and use your unique life to help others find their path.

The mechanics of this aren't as important. A great musician can pick up a stick and a can and make you dance. It's the desire to want others to dance that's your job, and it's the development of the skills and talents to make and keep a rhythm that are your skills to practice.

That's what goes into your unique voice.

Chris Brogan is a *New York Times* bestselling author of eight books and counting. He's the CEO of Owner Media Group and a highly sought-after international keynote speaker. Learn more at http://chrisbrogan.com.

MATTHEW TURNER, AKA TURNDOG
The Reluctant Author

Podcasting, as I've mentioned, can be an amazing tool for meeting new people who you normally wouldn't have access to. When I met Matthew Turner, I have to say it was a unique experience for sure. Matthew approached me about an ambitious project he was doing to interview hundreds of entrepreneurs about their "Successful Mistake" for a book of the same name.

Matthew had been a previous guest on my show as it was gaining momentum, so I was honored to be included as one of the people he would feature in his book. However, there's a little more you need to know about Matthew and my relationship with him.

He's the reason I was able to complete this work. If you recall earlier in the book I talked about a complete meltdown I had where Brother John's comments derailed me. It was talking to Matthew that helped me to understand that my little episode was normal and that I had in that moment become a writer. Matthew is a masterful storyteller, a talented author, and a dear friend. I loved how Matthew discovered his voice so let's get right into his story.

My name is Matthew Turner and I'm an author who writes books that are more than 60,000 words long, but had you told my younger self I would one day be capable of that, I'd have said you were insane. Because the truth is, I didn't enjoy writing during my teenage years, and I wasn't a fan of reading, either. Grammar and spelling quickly became a cause of anxiety during school, and even today the rules that we're told are so important continue to escape me.

Yet here I am, a fully fledged writer of novels, business books, guides, and a few hundred articles. How the heck did this happen?

Story…

It's as simple as that simplistic word that you first heard as a small child. Those who loved you read stories to you before bed, and those stories formed the basis of your favorite movies and shows.

Story… a word we all know well, but too few embrace.

After all, I fought story's power for years, associating it with my less than stellar grammar. But at the age twenty-one I fell in and out of love with a girl for the first time, and in a bid to overcome the pain of this breakup, I wrote about my thoughts, my feelings, and a few ideas that rumbled within.

These thoughts manifested into a story, and this story eventually transformed into my first novel. And although I wasn't too sure how it came to be, I one day held a real book that I had written in my bare hands.

How?

Story… my love for storytelling that has always been there, but neglected for so long.

Because all of a sudden I looked back on my youth and considered my wayward imagination, creative tendencies, and the inner monologues I'd have whilst having a shower or before slipping into a deep sleep.

A force awoke within me, but it wasn't something I created in my early twenties, rather one that had always been there. It just needed to be re-discovered after misplacing it around my ninth birthday.

And with it, my life changed forever because I suddenly needed storytelling in my life: to tell my own story, to listen to other people's, to make new ones, and reinvent the old.

More books… my own business… podcasting and interviewing… and standing on stage so I could deliver a tale or two. A rumble grew into a full on tumble, and not only has my love for storytelling grown ever since, it's taken over my world and become its central force.

I call myself a writer these days, but the truth is I'm a storyteller who just so happens to put words onto paper. But I don't want you to think that a story is a book, or vice versa. A story is about whatever medium best helps you share your tale with those who need it.

I love to write, but I also love to stand on stage and share my worth with a real crowd that you can see, hear, and practically touch. I don't see speaking on stage as a talk, rather a performance that requires a different twist each and every time.

Because the words you place onto paper aren't as simple as the person on the other end reading them. It's about doing everything in your power to make them feel something.

And I take this obsession to make folk feel onto the stage, as I do when I jump on an interview for a podcast, or in front of a camera. A story is a story is a story, no matter how you tell it.

It's about making the other person feel, although this in itself is neither easy to master nor easy to face.

Because it requires a voice… your voice… and discovering your voice is possibly the hardest thing you'll ever do.

It's scary, and I spent years terrified I'd never find it, or that even if I did, it wouldn't be good enough. Because to write is easy, but to do so in a manner that makes someone feel… now that's a different question altogether.

It's also easy to stand on stage and talk, but to perform it in a way that forces the hairs on people's necks to rise to attention… oh my, this is a different notion entirely.

But it's this that happens to be the beauty of story, because so long as your voice is the most important aspect of all, it means you have a role to play; maybe not in everybody's life, but in some.

And although I used to fear this entire notion, I no longer do because I appreciate that a voice is developed over time, not simply found one day by chance. You earn it by turning up, again and again, be it through writing, speaking, or performing.

So if all of this hinges on you doing… and doing… and doing some more, then the real key is simply beginning in the first place.

I speak to people each week who sense their story isn't worthy enough to tell, but the wonderful nature of your story is that it is your story; it's a unique fingerprint that sets you apart from everyone else, as is your voice and the way in which you tell it.

The moment you decide to tell your story isn't the end point, it's the beginning. It's the period in time when you decide to embrace storytelling, go in search of your voice, and craft it through hard work; not in the hope that it will one day fall into your lap.

It's this stubbornness to push through fear that helped me embrace storytelling in the first place, and rediscover a passion I had forgotten existed altogether. It's also this stubbornness to push through fear that has guided me along each stage of this journey I'm on ever since.

I continue to feel like I've only just scratched the surface, but this doesn't worry me anymore. I love it because it proves how I have so much still to look forward to.

So although I have to pinch myself some days, I am indeed a writer and storyteller.

My teenage self would find this hard to believe, but the signs were there all along. I believe the signs are there in us all, and for most it's a matter of time before they figure this out and let the art of story into their lives.

Because we all have a story, after all, and wouldn't it be a shame if we never shared it?

Chapter 11

UNDERSTANDING
YOUR IMPORTANCE

From *Hamilton, So Listen to My Declaration*:
ELIZA/ANGELICA/PEGGY
"We hold these truths to be self-evident
That all men are created equal"
ANGELICA
And when I meet Thomas Jefferson
COMPANY
Unh!
ANGELICA
I'm 'a compel him to include women in the sequel!
WOMEN
Work!

Work Indeed! I've had too many conversations with my sistas (yeah, I meant it to be spelled that way) about their men not being comfortable with how they express themselves and often it's because they feel threatened by the freedom they show in their self-expression.

I thought it was a black thing, but through conversations, observations, and growing my circle of influence I've learned this attitude transcends race. On a side note: I've found that most issues transcend race.

There's another side to this coin before I go too far into this. Some women also impose these limits of knowing their value and underestimating their importance on themselves. I'm not sure why this happens and I'm sure there are a multitude of reasons, but I've seen it and it's something I also hope this chapter can address, or at least give some alternative ways of thinking about self-worth.

Let's Take a Few Notes

What makes you feel valuable? Do me a favor and grab a pen and write it down.

Do you base your value on what people say to you or what they say about how you look, sound, or act?

What about how they treat you?

Would you treat yourself better if you felt more valuable?

It's been said so many different ways in every self-help book I've read about self-worth and self-love, but I think our constitution says it best. All men [mankind] are created equal.

Being raised by a woman, and a very strong one at that, I can't understand how women are so undervalued. Of course, men, we need to understand our value as well, but for women I think it's a little more of a challenge.

"When you don't feel your value, it's extremely hard to find your voice." ~Vernon Ross

For women, however, I think it's a little more difficult because they're the nurturers who give reassurance to the family and are so busy taking care of everyone else and making sure the family is taken care of that they rarely take that same time to make sure they feel okay about themselves.

I think that is what causes at least a portion of the problem when you start the conversation about not understanding your value. When you don't feel your value it's extremely hard to find your voice.

When I talk about finding your voice, I don't want you to think that I'm just talking about being on stage or being behind a microphone or being on video. A lot of this is within relationships, when you find your voice to communicate exactly what you think or how you feel, your dreams and desire and ambitions without fear of put downs or ridicule or rejection.

Women are taught from a very young age to put other things and other people above and before themselves and when you're trying to find your voice it's very hard to put other people's feelings and sensibilities in front of your own without losing your voice.

One would think that you would have to be selfish, but that's not what it is at all. I think you have to be selfless and understand that by expressing yourself you're not hurting the other person, you're actually helping them understand how you feel and therefore gaining more understanding about yourself in the process.

Finding your voice and the power in your own words to be able to express yourself fully as a person is what I think it means to master your message, and for women I think these truths are self-evident.

Chapter 12

BRINGING THE MESSAGE HOME

Writing this work has been an amazing experience for me and I hope you've enjoyed reading it as much as I've loved writing it.

One of the many things I would have you focus on during your journey to finding your voice would be to work on your mindset. How you think and how the internal conversations you have will affect your level of success and how long you actually maintain it. Remember, internal conversations can build you up, but they can also tear you down.

It's really hard work to be yourself. We have messages all around us showing off others who seem more connected, smarter, and what appears to be better prepared for just about everything we're attempting to do. At times it seems like you're falling through life with no one listening. Yes, finding your voice is equally as challenging, but if you read the stories in this work and apply the lessons contained I know you will start to discover your own story.

It's All About Style

One of the last things I think I developed was style and what I like to call *flow*. I like to define *style* as the way you navigate through life and deliver your message. Each person's style is going to be different even if you're imitating someone else like I did that first time I had to perform in front of a crowd.

If you've ever watched a TED Talk you'll know what I'm referring to with the imitation game. TED speakers receive training on how to present and how to command the stage. It's great training and I hope to one day grace the stage and talk about how I overcame my fear that first time and how it's changed my life. I digress. Watch five random, lesser known talks and you'll see a very recognizable style to each speaker.

They aren't all exactly the same, but you can tell each speaker was obviously coached to present a certain way so they remain within their allotted eighteen minutes. The same goes for their delivery. It's the same pace across the stage and the same praying hands pose you see so many TED speakers take.

I could easily sound like I'm slamming TED for creating a template for new and seasoned speakers to follow. But I'm not. I think it's great, actually, and I encourage you to watch as many TED Talks as you can! While you're watching, stand up and imitate the speaker's mannerisms and speech patterns and model your talk, your contribution to a meeting, or how you communicate on a webinar using the TED Talk speaker as a point of reference.

This method is powerful because it gets you talking out loud and practicing what you're going to say. Talking to yourself will help you to understand how you sound, what it feels like to deliver your message no matter the situation you have to deliver it in.

We have a choice to hide behind excuses, fear, and small-minded thinking, or we can step up and claim our greatness. I want you to step into the power that you have in finding your voice and ultimately mastering your message.

ABOUT THE AUTHOR

Vernon Ross is an author, internationally known podcaster, and digital strategist. As an inspirational speaker whose insights are based on real world experience, he takes his message on the road to universities, national conferences, and workshops across the country. Ross serves as an adjunct professor at the University of Missouri, St. Louis. He resides in the St. Louis area with his family.

BIBLIOGRAPHY

Beck, Julie. "Life's Stories: How You Arrange the Plot Points
    of Your Life into a Narrative Can Shape Who You
    Are—and Is a Fundamental Part of Being Human." The
    Atlantic. Atlantic Media Company, 10 Aug. 2015. Web.
    21 July 2016. Quote by Jonathan Adler, an assistant
    professor of psychology at Olin College of Engineering

Williamson, Marianne. *A Return to Love: Reflections on
    the Principles of a Course in Miracles.* New York, NY:
    HarperCollins, 1992. Print.

Maxwell, John C. *Intentional Living: Choosing a Life That
    Matters.* N.p.: n.p., n.d. Print.

Gladwell, Malcolm. "Chapter 2 The 10,000 Hour Rule."
    Outliers: The Story of Success. New York: Little, Brown,
    2008. N. pag. Print.

A free eBook edition is available with the purchase of this book.

To claim your free eBook edition:

1. Download the Shelfie app.
2. Write your name in upper case in the box.
3. Use the Shelfie app to submit a photo.
4. Download your eBook to any device.

Shelfie

A free eBook edition is available
with the purchase of this print book.

CLEARLY PRINT YOUR NAME ABOVE IN UPPER CASE

Instructions to claim your free eBook edition:
1. Download the Shelfie app for Android or iOS
2. Write your name in **UPPER CASE** above
3. Use the Shelfie app to submit a photo
4. Download your eBook to any device

Print & Digital Together Forever.

Snap a photo

Free eBook

Read anywhere

Morgan James
Speakers Group

We connect Morgan James published
authors with live and online events
and audiences whom will benefit
from their expertise.

Printed in the USA
CPSIA information can be obtained
at www.ICGtesting.com
JSHW082358140824
68134JS00020B/2139